※ Smithsonian

A WORLD WAR II

BY ELIZABETH RAUM

TIMELINE

CAPSTONE PRESS
a capstone imprint

Capstone Press
1710 Roe Crest Drive
North Mankato, Minnesota 56003
www.capstonepub.com

The name of the Smithsonian Institution and the sunburst logo
are registered trademarks of the Smithsonian Institution.
For more information, please visit www.si.edu.

Our very special thanks to F. Robert van der Linden, chairman of the Aeronautics
Division at the National Air and Space Museum, Smithsonian Institution, for his
curatorial review. Capstone would also like to thank Kealy Wilson, Smithsonian
Institution Product Development Manager, and the following at Smithsonian
Enterprises: Ellen Nanney, Licensing Manager; Brigid Ferraro, Vice President,
Education and Consumer Products; Carol LeBlanc, Senior Vice President,
Education and Consumer Products.

Library of Congress Cataloging-in-Publication Data
Raum, Elizabeth.
A World War II timeline / by Elizabeth Raum.
pages cm. — (Smithsonian war timelines)
Includes index.
Summary: "A photographic timeline of World War II"—Provided by publisher.
ISBN 978-1-4765-4158-7 (library binding)
ISBN 978-1-4765-5178-4 (paperback)
1. World War, 1939–1945—Chronology—Juvenile literature. I. Title.
D743.7.R39 2014
940.53—dc23   2013032306

Editorial Credits
Kristen Mohn, editor; Ted Williams, designer; Svetlana Zhurkin, media researcher;
Kathy McColley, production specialist

Photo Credits
DVIC: NARA, cover (background, bottom middle, and bottom right), back cover,
1, 3, 4, 6–7 (back), 7, 10–11 (back), 12–13 (back), 13, 14–15 (back), 14, 15 (top),
16–17 (back), 19, 22–23 (back), 22, 25 (bottom), 26–27 (back), 26 (right), 27
(right), 31 (bottom), 32–33 (back), 34–35 (back), 34 (left), 35, 36–37 (bottom), 36,
37, 38–39 (back), 38, 39 (right), 40–41 (back), 40, 41, 42–43 (back), 42, 43, 44
(top left, top right, and bottom left); Library of Congress, cover (bottom left), 6, 8,
9, 10 (top), 12, 16 (bottom), 20 (left), 23 (bottom), 24, 27 (left), 28–29 (back), 28,
29 (top), 30–31 (back), 30 (left), 31 (top), 32, 39 (left), 44 (bottom right); National
Museum of American History, Behring Center, Smithsonian Institution, 26 (left);
Newscom: akg-images, 33, 34 (right), ITAR-TASS, 30 (right), UIG Universal
Images Group/Mondadori Collection, 29 (bottom); Shutterstock: Andrey_Kuzmin,
20–21 (back), Deborah Benbrook, 18 (bottom), Gelia, 18–19 (back), 47, IanC66,
15 (bottom), Jaime Pharr, 25 (top), Jan Kranendonk, 10 (bottom), Neftali, 11,
Pavel L Photo and Video, 24–25 (back), Timothy R. Nichols, 18 (top); Wikipedia,
16 (top), Adam Carr, 20 (right), David Shankbone, 23 (top), Karsten Sperling, 17,
National Archives of Canada, 8–9 (back)

Printed in the United States of America.
0562

TABLE OF CONTENTS

WORLD WAR II

It was the "war to end all wars." The death and damage of the Great War (1914–1918) was so huge that everyone hoped there would never be another like it. But the treaties that ended the first world war did not bring lasting peace. Instead they led to another world war—World War II—that was even more costly than the first.

The Treaty of Versailles officially ended World War I in 1919. By signing the treaty, Germany accepted harsh punishments, lost territory, and was forced to accept guilt for starting the war. Germany also had to repay France and other countries for damage caused by the war. This was a major blow to the German economy. Prices went up and money lost its value. People struggled just to get enough to eat.

These difficult conditions led to the rise of Adolf Hitler, the leader of the Nazi Party. Hitler was a powerful speaker who blamed France and Great Britain for Germany's woes. The Nazi Party promised to rebuild Germany and make it stronger than ever. Throughout the 1930s the Nazis gained power. Hitler began to plan a German takeover of Europe.

Italy also felt cheated at the end of World War I. Italy had agreed to help France and England fight Germany in exchange for territory along the Austria-Hungary border.

However, at war's end Italy gained little new territory. And more than 1.4 million Italians had died in the war. Unrest grew. Benito Mussolini became the country's leader in 1922. As dictator of Italy, he sided with Hitler and the Germans.

In addition to the problems created by the Treaty of Versailles, the world slid into the Great Depression. Factories shut down, people lost jobs, and prices increased throughout the world. The Great Depression began in the United States in 1929, but quickly spread to Europe and Asia. Japan was especially hard-hit. China, one of Japan's trading partners, refused to buy Japanese goods, and eventually Japan invaded China.

Meanwhile, Germany began to seize territory in Austria. No one wanted another war, but France and Great Britain did not want Germany to regain its former strength and territory. Was it already too late? The seeds of a new world war had begun to grow.

From the rise of Hitler to the Allies' final victory, this book presents a step-by-step timeline of the most important events of World War II. Together the events tell the dramatic story of the fight to stop the evil that threatened the world.

THE CRISIS BEGINS

Japan invades Manchuria, China, seeking additional land for its growing population. Manchuria has farmland, forests, and other natural resources.

1931

1932

1933

Jan. 30

Adolf Hitler is appointed chancellor of Germany. The following year he becomes president as well and calls himself Führer. He bribes German lawmakers into granting him the full powers of a dictator. Soon after, Hitler establishes the first concentration camps to imprison people opposed to Nazi policies. He declares, "I will go down as the greatest German in history."

1935

Nov. 8

Franklin Delano Roosevelt is elected president of the United States.

Sept. 15

Germany enacts the anti-Jewish Nuremberg Laws. Jews are no longer considered German citizens. Marriage between Jews and non-Jews is illegal.

Oct. 3

Benito Mussolini, Italy's dictator, invades Abyssinia (Ethiopia). He believes that Abyssinia's natural resources will help solve Italy's economic troubles.

1936–1939

Civil war breaks out in Spain. Germany and Italy support General Francisco Franco, who leads forces to overthrow the Spanish government. Franco becomes Spain's new leader. He supports Hitler and Mussolini during the early stages of WWII.

Oct. 25

Mussolini (left) and Hitler form an alliance by signing the Rome-Berlin Axis. They sign the Pact of Steel in 1939, which links the two countries more officially.

March 12

Germany annexes Austria in a bloodless invasion.

1936   1938

March 7

German troops occupy the Rhineland, an area under Allied control since WWI.

Nov. 25

Germany and Japan sign the Anti-Comintern Pact. They pledge to support each other against attack by the Soviet Union. The Soviet Union, founded in 1922 when several republics joined together as a Communist state, supports China. Italy signs the Anti-Comintern Pact one year later.

Sept. 30

Great Britain, France, and Italy permit Germany to annex lands in the Sudetenland, which is what Germany calls the German-speaking parts of Czechoslovakia. Hitler pledges to take no more territory in Europe.

BROKEN PROMISES

May

Despite his pledge to take no more territory, Hitler orders German troops to occupy all of Czechoslovakia. He threatens Poland. Earlier, British Prime Minister Neville Chamberlain had promised to aid Poland if Germany attacked.

August

Albert Einstein, a German physicist who had moved to the U.S., sends President Roosevelt a letter warning that a new discovery, nuclear fission, could lead to the development of atomic bombs. Einstein wrote, "A single bomb of this type, carried by boat and exploded in a port, might very well destroy the whole port together with some of the surrounding territory." Einstein sent a total of four letters. Eventually Roosevelt set up the Manhattan Project in the U.S., which led to the development of the atomic bomb.

Sept. 1

Germany attacks Poland in a blitzkrieg ("lightning war") using more than 2,000 tanks and 1,000 planes. Great Britain and France demand that Germany withdraw. Hitler refuses.

1939

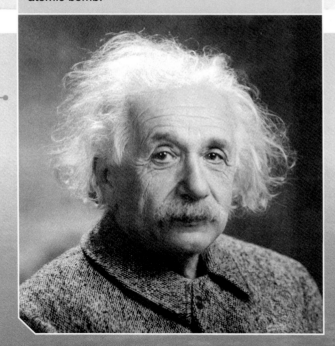

Aug. 19–23

Germany and the Soviet Union sign the German-Soviet Pact. It allows Germany to sell goods to the Soviets in exchange for raw materials. They promise not to attack each other for 10 years.

Sept. 3

Great Britain, France, Australia, and New Zealand declare war on Germany, but they do not aid Poland. Meanwhile, a German U-boat sinks the British passenger liner *Athenia*, killing 112 passengers. Britain sees this as the start of submarine warfare.

Sept. 17

Upon the orders of Soviet leader Joseph Stalin, Foreign Minister Vyacheslav Molotov declares that Poland no longer exists. Stalin sends Soviet troops to occupy eastern Poland as part of the German-Soviet Pact. German troops occupy western Poland.

Sept. 5

President Roosevelt declares that the United States will not take sides and will remain neutral.

THE PHONY WAR

October

Now that Poland is in German hands, the Nazis force Warsaw's 400,000 Jews into a ghetto, which consists of about 10 streets. Germans seize the Jews' furniture and personal belongings.

Nov. 4

The U.S. begins sending war supplies to France and Britain. Despite its neutrality, the U.S. government wants to aid the Allies.

September

People in Great Britain and France expect war. A long waiting period begins. The following eight months are called the Phony War or the Twilight War. Most adults and children in England are given gas masks to protect their lungs in case the Germans use poison gas. British troops plant mines in the English Channel to protect against German U-boats. British planes drop millions of leaflets over German cities urging peace. More than 3 million people—mostly children—leave British cities for safer places in the countryside.

Sweden, Norway, and Denmark declare neutrality.

British naval mine

THE TWO SIDES

Germany began World War II. Italy and Japan joined with Germany to form the Axis Forces. Opposing the Axis were the Allied Forces led by the United Kingdom, France, and eventually the Soviet Union and the United States. All the original members of the United Nations were considered Allies. They included Australia, Belgium, Canada, China, Costa Rica, Cuba, Czechoslovakia, Dominican Republic, El Salvador, Greece, Guatemala, Haiti, Honduras, India, Luxembourg, the Netherlands, New Zealand, Nicaragua, Norway, Panama, Poland, South Africa, and Yugoslavia. During the war, the Philippines, Mexico, Ethiopia, Iraq, Free French, and Free Danes joined the Allies.

Nov. 8

Johann Georg Elser, a German Communist, plants a bomb at a Nazi party meeting in Munich. He wants to kill Hitler, who is speaking there. The bomb kills eight and wounds 63, but Hitler escapes. The Nazis blame the attempt on British spies. Elser is killed in a death camp in 1945.

Dec. 14

The Soviet Union is expelled from the League of Nations after refusing to halt the invasion of Finland. The League of Nations, founded in 1920 as a place to resolve international disputes, cannot solve this one. Japan and Germany left the league in 1933. Italy left in 1937.

Nov. 30

Soviet troops invade Finland. At the end of a four-month war, more than 400,000 Finns lose their homes and land to the Soviets.

11

Jan. 8

The British government begins rationing food. Less than one-third of British food is homegrown. Most foods come from other countries, but German ships are disrupting supplies. Every person receives a book of ration tickets. A typical weekly allowance includes one fresh egg, 4 oz. bacon and margarine, 2 oz. tea and butter, 1 oz. cheese, and 8 oz. sugar. Many British people begin growing "victory gardens" to supply their own food.

April 9

German warships deliver thousands of German troops to Norway. Norway refuses to surrender. German paratroopers invade and establish a government friendly to Hitler. German forces occupy Denmark. The Danish king surrenders.

1940

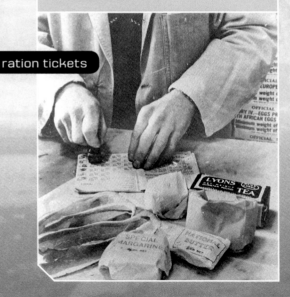

ration tickets

March

France and Britain want to send troops to Finland, but the Swedish government won't let them cross Sweden.

Mid-April

British and French forces reach Norway. They begin an attack on the German forces, but withdraw when they receive news of attacks on France.

Belgian refugees

May 10

Winston Churchill replaces Neville Chamberlain as prime minister of Great Britain.

May 26–June 4

German troops force Allied soldiers back toward the French coast at Dunkirk. The British send about 900 ships to carry more than 200,000 British troops and more than 100,000 French and Belgian troops across the English Channel to safety in Great Britain.

May 10

Germany launches bombing attacks on Allied troops fighting in Europe. They invade the Netherlands, Belgium, and France.

May 14

Germans bomb Rotterdam in the Netherlands. Queen Wilhelmina and the Dutch government escape to London. The Netherlands surrenders to Germany the next day. Belgium surrenders May 28.

FRANCE FALLS;
BRITAIN UNDER ATTACK

June 14

German troops enter Paris. France surrenders on June 22. Germany orders the French Army to disband and makes France pay for the cost of occupation. Hitler visits Paris on June 28.

June 18

Winston Churchill tells the British people, "The Battle of France is over. The Battle of Britain is about to begin."

June–August

The Soviet Union annexes Latvia, Lithuania, and Estonia.

Hitler in Paris

June 10

Italy declares war on France and Britain.

July–October

U-boats attack Allied convoys in the North Atlantic.

1940

Sept. 7

The Blitz begins. The Luftwaffe bombs central London. Thousands seek shelter in London's Underground stations. By the time the Blitz ends in May 1941, 43,000 British civilians are dead. Thousands of buildings are destroyed. Churchill inspires courage when he says, "We will fight [the Germans] on the beaches … we shall fight in the fields and in the streets … we shall never surrender."

July 10

The Battle of Britain begins. The Luftwaffe, Germany's air force, disrupts British shipping and tries to destroy the Royal Air Force (RAF). Hitler expects a swift victory, but Britain's new radar system gives the British advance warnings. RAF Hurricane and Spitfire fighter planes perform better than the German Messerschmitt 109E. By October the RAF has lost 1,023 planes and the Luftwaffe 1,887.

Spitfire

Sept. 13

Mussolini sends Italian troops to Egypt to claim land that was once Italian. British troops protecting the Suez Canal force the Italians to surrender five months later.

Oct. 28

Italy invades Greece.

Sept. 27

Germany, Italy, and Japan sign the Tripartite Pact. They promise to help one another in case of attack. Hungary, Romania, and Slovakia sign in late November.

Oct. 29

Military draft begins in the U.S.

BREAKING CODES,
BREAKING PACTS

January

Japanese Admiral Isoroku Yamamoto begins planning the Pearl Harbor attack.

Nazis develop the Final Solution, a plan to kill all the Jews in Europe.

1941

January–February

War in northern Africa heats up. British and Australian troops battle Italians in Libya, Egypt, and Ethiopia. Hitler sends General Erwin Rommel and German troops to help Italy seize the Suez Canal and set up a pro-German government in oil-rich Iraq.

March–April

British forces reach Greece to offer protection against the Italians.

April–June

Pro-German forces cut off the Allies' Iraqi oil supply. Indian troops join British forces in overthrowing the pro-German government and regaining Iraqi oil.

March

The U.S. begins the Lend-Lease Program to give ammunition and war supplies to Great Britain. Roosevelt tells Congress that the Allies are fighting for four freedoms: "the freedom of speech, the freedom of worship, the freedom from want, and the freedom from fear."

May 9

The British Navy captures a German U-boat off the coast of Iceland and finds a working Enigma machine.

April 6

Germany, Italy, Bulgaria, and Hungary invade Greece and Yugoslavia. By the end of the month, Axis powers occupy the region.

BREAKING THE ENIGMA CODE

The German military used the Enigma cipher machine to send and receive messages. The Enigma looked like a typewriter. A series of rotating wheels and rotors swapped one letter for another. Each day operators set the switches to a new pre-arranged position and then typed a message. The message made no sense until an operator at the other end retyped the message into the machine to decipher it. After the British Navy found the Enigma, they sent it to Bletchley Park where British code breakers cracked the code. Historians claim that breaking the Enigma cipher shortened the war by two years and saved countless lives.

June 22

Hitler breaks the Soviet-German Pact by sending 3 million troops into the Soviet Union. His goal is to destroy the Communist government and to eliminate all Soviet Jews. Italy, Romania, Finland, and Hungary declare war on the Soviet Union.

May 24–27

The German battleship *Bismarck* sinks the British battleship *Hood* in the North Atlantic. In turn, the British fleet sinks the *Bismarck*. This victory opens up Allied shipping routes.

MASS MURDERS

Nazis order all Jews in Germany, Bohemia, and Moravia to wear a yellow Star of David on their clothing. All European Jews are in danger.

July

Nazi death squads murder 5,000 Jews in Vilna, Lithuania. Mass murders occur in Russia and Croatia. Jews in Poland, Germany, and France are forced into ghettos or concentration camps.

Japan occupies the French colony of Indochina. The U.S cuts off oil supplies to Japan.

Aug. 8

Germany begins the siege of Leningrad (St. Petersburg). It will last 900 days.

1941

July 12

British and Soviet leaders become allies against Germany.

August–September

Germans destroy the city of Smolensk, 220 miles (354 kilometers) southwest of Moscow, and circle Kiev in Ukraine. Germans capture 600,000 prisoners and 2,500 Soviet tanks. Nazi "mobile killing units" kill 34,000 Kiev Jews at a ravine called Babi Yar.

Sept. 3

Nazis use gas chambers at Auschwitz to kill Russian prisoners of war (POWs). By 1944 about 1.6 million people are killed at Auschwitz including political prisoners, Jews, and Roma (Gypsies).

Oct. 16

Hideki Tojo becomes the Japanese prime minister and orders an attack against the U.S. to take place Dec. 7. Japanese Army and Navy officers prepare for war against the U.S.

November

The U.S. orders Japan to get out of China and Indochina. Japan sends representatives to Washington in attempts to avoid war.

Dec. 7

Japanese bombers attack the U.S. fleet at Pearl Harbor in Hawaii. The surprise attack kills 2,403 Americans, destroys 188 aircraft, and sinks 21 ships.

Dec. 11

Germany and Italy declare war on the U.S.

Oct. 31

A German U-boat torpedoes the U.S. Navy warship *Reuben James* in the North Atlantic, killing 115 sailors. It is the first U.S. ship sunk in the war.

Dec. 5

The Soviet Army launches a counterattack and stops the German invasion at the gates of Moscow. Britain declares war on Finland, Romania, and Hungary, all now in German control.

Dec. 8

The U.S. and Britain declare war on Japan.

Roosevelt signs declaration of war

19

January–February

Axis planes carry out 498 air raids over the island of Malta, the only British naval base in the Mediterranean Sea.

Jan. 16–19

Hitler fires 30 top generals who urge withdrawal from the Soviet Union.

1942

Jan. 2

Japanese forces capture the city of Manila in the Philippines, a U.S. possession. Japan plans to create an empire in the Pacific and take over all European and American territories. U.S. and Filipino forces, under U.S. General Douglas MacArthur, withdraw from Manila to the Bataan Peninsula.

Jan. 20

Nazi Party and German government officials meet at a mansion in Wannsee, a Berlin suburb, to discuss the "Final Solution to the Jewish Question." They decide how to destroy Europe's 11 million Jews: send them to concentration camps and force them to work; those who survive hard labor will be gassed.

Jan. 26

First U.S. troops arrive in Britain to prepare to fight. By the end of the war, 1.5 million American servicemen will have been stationed in or have passed through Great Britain.

Feb. 23

A Japanese submarine surfaces off the coast of California and shells an oil refinery near Santa Barbara. This is the first attack on the continental U.S.

March 11

President Roosevelt orders General MacArthur to leave the Bataan Peninsula. MacArthur leaves behind 80,000 troops but promises, "I shall return." On March 17 Roosevelt appoints MacArthur commander of Allied forces in the Southwest Pacific.

February–March

Japanese troops invade Singapore and the Dutch East Indies (Indonesia) and occupy Burma (Myanmar).

Feb. 27–29

In the Battle of the Java Sea, Japan defeats the Allies.

alliances in 1942

Allied Controlled
Axis Controlled
Neutral

SOVIET UNION
CHINA   JAPAN
PHILIPPINES
Pacific Ocean

SWEDEN   FINLAND   SOVIET UNION
Atlantic Ocean   NORWAY
North Sea   ESTONIA
    LATVIA
    DENMARK   LITHUANIA
IRELAND   NETHERLANDS   PRUSSIA
GREAT BRITAIN   POLAND
BELGIUM   GERMANY   SLOVAKIA
SWITZERLAND   HUNGARY
FRANCE   ROMANIA   Black Sea
    ITALY   YUGOSLAVIA BULGARIA
PORTUGAL
SPAIN   TURKEY
    GREECE   SYRIA
    PALESTINE   TRANS-JORDAN
MOROCCO   TUNISIA   Mediterranean Sea
    ALGERIA
    LIBYA   EGYPT

TURNING
POINTS

April 18

U.S. Army Air Force bombers under the command of Lt. Col. Jimmy Doolittle bomb Japan for the first time. They take off from the aircraft carrier USS *Hornet* 800 miles (1,287 km) from Tokyo.

April

More than 120,000 Americans of Japanese ancestry are moved from their West Coast homes to internment camps in the U.S. Half are children. Many are held for four years.

April 9

U.S. and Filipino forces on the Bataan Peninsula surrender to the Japanese—80,000 are taken prisoner. Japanese officers force them to march 65 miles (105 km) north to a POW camp. More than 10,000 men die on the Bataan Death March.

May–June

In North Africa Rommel defeats the British in the Battle of Gazala. The British lose the port city of Tobruk to the Germans.

May 30

The RAF sends 1,000 planes to bomb the German city of Cologne and shut down German chemical and machine tool factories. The raid leaves 469 Germans dead and 45,000 homeless.

June

Japanese troops land on the Aleutian Islands, a U.S. territory located between Russia and Alaska.

June 25

President Roosevelt appoints General Dwight Eisenhower commander of U.S. forces in Europe.

July–September

Nazi SS (special paramilitary) units and German police deport about 300,000 Jews from the Warsaw ghetto to Treblinka death camp. By September only 70,000 Jews remain in the ghetto.

May 4–8

In the Battle of the Coral Sea, U.S. naval forces stop the Japanese fleet. It is the first naval battle in history conducted solely by airpower where neither fleet can see its opponent.

June 4–7

During the Battle of Midway, the U.S. fleet sinks four Japanese aircraft carriers and prevents the occupation of the strategic island. The victory is aided by the breaking of the Japanese military code. It is the turning point of the war in the Pacific.

June–July

Germans attack southern Ukraine to capture oil fields in Sevastopol. They capture 90,000 Soviet troops.

LOSSES MOUNT
ON BOTH SIDES

Aug. 7

11,000 U.S. Marines land at Guadalcanal, the largest of the Solomon Islands, to stop the Japanese from building an airstrip. Fighting continues on land and at sea until February when Japanese forces give up. Deaths on the island include 1,600 Americans and 24,000 Japanese. At sea each side loses 24 ships and thousands of sailors.

Aug. 19

Allied troops raid German-held Dieppe in northern France. The Germans take 2,190 Allies prisoner.

Aug. 29

Japan won't let Red Cross ships deliver supplies to U.S. POWs.

1942

Aug. 13

President Roosevelt approves the Manhattan Project, the top-secret effort to develop an atomic bomb.

German POWs

Aug. 23

Germany begins a massive attack on Stalingrad (Volgograd). German bombs kill 40,000 civilians in one of the most brutal battles of the war. Fighting intensifies throughout the fall and winter. The German Army surrenders to the Soviets in January 1943 and 91,000 Germans become POWs. The Battle of Stalingrad is a turning point of the war in Europe.

DEATH CAMPS

Between 1933 and 1945 Nazi Germany established as many as 20,000 prison camps. They imprisoned Jews, Roma (Gypsies), POWs, and others who challenged Hitler's policies. Many prisoners died from overwork, starvation, and disease. In 1941 the Nazis created death camps in Poland. Gas chambers at Chelmno, Belzec, Sobibor, Treblinka, and Auschwitz used poison gas to murder prisoners. Between 1.1 million and 1.5 million people were murdered at Auschwitz, 750,000 to 900,000 at Treblinka, and at least 600,000 at Belzec. Most of the victims were Jews.

Auschwitz memorial

Sept. 2

Nazis kill 50,000 Jews in Poland's Warsaw ghetto.

Nov. 11

German and Italian troops begin occupying the portion of France not already under German control.

British General Bernard L. Montgomery

October–November

Allies win a decisive battle against Rommel and the German Afrika Korps at El Alamein in Egypt. Rommel retreats to Tunisia. On Nov. 8, in Operation Torch, 107,000 Allied troops land on the North African coast, beginning the final stage of the war in Africa.

Dec. 17

British foreign secretary Anthony Eden makes the first public statement about Nazi death camps. Belgium, Czechoslovakia, Greece, Luxembourg, the Netherlands, Norway, Poland, the United States, Great Britain, the Soviet Union, Yugoslavia, and the French National Committee condemn Germany.

Jan. 18–21

Jewish resisters in Poland's Warsaw ghetto, the ZOB (Jewish Fighting Organization), attack German SS units as they deport more Jews. The ZOB stops the deportations. SS units respond by killing 1,000 Jews. Since 1941 young Jews have formed secret resistance groups to fight the Nazis.

Feb. 7

President Roosevelt appoints General Eisenhower commander of Allied operations in North Africa. The war in North Africa ends May 13 with the capture of 240,000 Axis soldiers in Tunisia.

March 2–4

U.S. planes sink 12 Japanese ships in the South Pacific.

1943

U.S. manufacturing surges ahead to produce war supplies, including 30,000 tanks and 83,000 planes. Shipyards build three merchant ships a day. Most factories operate three shifts a day. By 1944 19 million women have entered the workforce to make up for the 12 million men and women serving in the military. Rosie the Riveter shows the important role women play.

Jan. 27

The U.S. launches bombing raids on Germany.

April 17

U.S. bombers attack aircraft factories in Bremen, Germany.

May 16–17

Royal Air Force Lancaster bombers, fitted with special "bouncing" bombs, attack and destroy two German dams while damaging a third.

May 11

U.S. troops land on Attu Island in the Aleutian Islands and defeat Japanese forces there after heavy fighting.

April 18

U.S. Army planes shoot down Japanese Admiral Yamamoto's plane over the Solomon Islands. Yamamoto was commander of Japan's Pacific fleet and planned the Pearl Harbor attack.

May 16

The Warsaw ghetto uprising ends in defeat. The Germans burn the ghetto and deport the remaining Jews. Some ZOB fighters escape and join other resistance groups.

ALLIES ADVANCE

May

German U-boats sink 34 Allied vessels, but they lose one-fifth of their U-boat fleet to Allied attack. The Battle of the Atlantic continues, but now Allies are in control.

July 5–Aug. 23

Despite losses in Stalingrad, Hitler sends troops and tanks to attack the city of Kursk. The battle involves 6,000 tanks, 4,000 planes, and German Panther and Tiger tanks with antitank mines. Soviet victory stops Germany's advance.

June 10

The U.S. agrees to bomb Germany by day and the RAF will bomb at night in Operation Pointblank. About 100,000 Allied crewmen are killed or captured during the bombings.

July 10

U.S. General George Patton leads an amphibious assault on the Italian island of Sicily. It takes three days to ferry 150,000 Allied troops to shore on amphibious landing crafts. On shore the Allies battle Italian and German troops. Sicily surrenders Aug. 17. Mainland Italy is the next goal.

July 24–Aug. 3

Allied bombing raids drop more than 8,000 tons of bombs on Hamburg, Germany. The ensuing firestorm kills an estimated 40,000 people.

Aug. 17

In the aerial Battle of Schweinfurt and Regensburg, the U.S. Army Air Force loses 60 bombers in an air raid, a loss of more than 20 percent. Most of the remaining bombers return damaged.

Sept. 5–16

U.S. paratroopers land in New Guinea. Australian and American troops capture two Japanese bases in the towns of Salamaua and Lae.

Sept. 25

Soviet troops recapture Smolensk.

July 25

Mussolini is forced out of power by his own government and imprisoned. German commandos rescue him in September from his mountain prison in the Apennines. With German help, he sets up a pro-German government in the northern Italian city of Salo.

Aug. 22

German troops withdraw from Kharkov, Ukraine.

Sept. 8

General Eisenhower announces Italy's surrender to the Allies. The next day Allied troops land at Salerno in southern Italy. German generals take control of Rome, Milan, Bologna, and Verona. Allied forces reach Naples by Oct. 1. Meanwhile, the Italians are divided. Many Italians fight side by side with the Allies against the Germans, but those loyal to Mussolini support the Germans.

Nov. 6

Soviet forces liberate Kiev from German control.

Sept. 13

The new Italian government declares war on Germany.

1943

Oct. 26

Japanese Emperor Hirohito states Japan's situation is "truly grave."

Nov. 6

Germany establishes the Gustav Line across Italy south of Rome to keep the Allies out of northern Italy. The line consists of defensive fortifications, including bunkers, gun turrets, and minefields.

Nov. 28

Stalin, Roosevelt, and Churchill (from left), known as the Big Three, meet in Tehran, Iran. They discuss ways to defeat the Nazis. They plan an invasion at Normandy, France. Stalin promises to fight Japan in return for U.S. help defeating the Germans in eastern Europe.

December

P-51B Mustangs are delivered to Allies in Europe. The P-51, one of the most effective fighters in the war, has large fuel tanks that allow it to reach any site in Europe. P-51s blast trains, ships, and enemy defenses. They are the first single-engine planes to reach Berlin.

Nov. 18–19

Allies begin continuous bombing of Berlin.

Nov. 20

The U.S. begins the Central Pacific Campaign by landing on Tarawa, a Japanese-held atoll in the Gilbert Islands. Marines defeat Japanese forces there after a 76-hour battle with heavy losses on both sides.

TERRITORY IN PACIFIC

1944

Jan. 22

Allies land at Anzio, Italy. Leaders hope to surprise the Germans at the Gustav Line. Landings take longer than expected, and German troops reach Anzio before the Allies can secure the beach. The Germans retreat, but not before the Allies suffer heavy losses.

Jan. 30

U.S. troops begin an invasion of the Japanese-held Marshall Islands. Within days the island of Kwajalein is secured.

Jan. 27

After 900 days the Siege of Leningrad ends. The people of Leningrad refused to surrender, despite freezing weather and a severe lack of food. At least 641,000 civilians died in the three-year battle against the Germans.

JAPANESE POW CAMPS

The Japanese held more than 27,000 Americans in POW camps in Japan, Taiwan, and other Japanese territories. Although the Red Cross sent food and medicine to the prisoners, Japanese officials kept it for themselves. POWs in Japan lacked adequate food, shelter, and medical care. Many worked 12-hour days in mines, fields, shipyards, and factories, but they received fewer than 600 calories of food a day. Many died of starvation and disease. Japanese soldiers shot and killed others. Forty percent of the American soldiers held in Japanese POW camps died before the war ended.

March 7

The Japanese launch an attack at Imphal in the hope of invading India, which is under British rule. British Commonwealth forces fight back. The battle ends in the largest defeat of the Japanese Army to that date with 30,000 soldiers killed.

February

U.S. planes bomb a Japanese naval base at Truk in the Caroline Islands. They destroy 200,000 tons of Japanese supplies. U.S. forces seize Eniwetok Atoll, the last Japanese-occupied Marshall Island, on Feb. 22.

March 15

Allies attack the Germans at Monte Cassino, an Italian mountain monastery between Naples and Anzio. The Allies' goal is to break through the Gustav Line and take control of Rome.

SETBACKS FOR
GERMANY AND JAPAN

April–August

Japan sends 600,000 troops to China to capture Allied airfields and establish a direct route across China to Southeast Asia. Fighting is fierce. The U.S. evacuates its airfields in China. By late August Japan defeats the Chinese forces.

May 11–18

The Allies break through the Gustav Line at Monte Cassino. The Germans withdraw. The Allies reach Rome on June 4.

1944

April 22

General MacArthur leads Allied forces against the Japanese in New Guinea. The Japanese hold out for three months before surrendering.

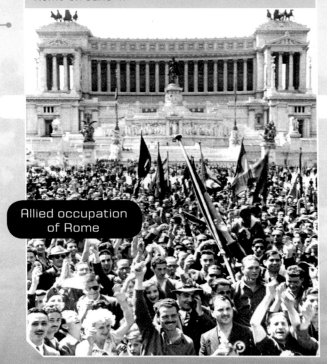

Allied occupation of Rome

May 15

Hungarian Jews are deported to gas chambers at Auschwitz. One-half of all Jews killed at Auschwitz were Hungarian.

Eisenhower gives D-Day orders to paratroopers

June 19

Japan suffers heavy losses in the Battle of the Philippine Sea. U.S. aircraft demolish Japan's carrier fleet and shoot down 480 Japanese combat planes while defending the liberation of Guam, a U.S. territory.

June 6

D-Day. For years Allied leaders knew they had to defeat Germany on the European mainland. They planned to cross the English Channel and retake France. Ships carry British, American, and Canadian troops across the channel the night of June 5. Amphibious craft carry troops to shore June 6. They surprise the Germans, who consider the site too rough for a landing. German snipers fire from hilltop bunkers and kill 9,000 of the 150,000 Allied soldiers on the beaches. Allied aircraft and French resistance fighters assist as troops move inland.

Summer

Stalin lays out a plan to use 2.4 million Russian troops to retake German-held areas of the eastern Soviet Union and to defeat Germans in Finland and Romania. Romania falls into Soviet hands Aug. 20. Finland surrenders Aug. 25. The Soviets prepare to enter Germany.

FRENCH RESISTANCE

Small groups of French men and women operated inside German-occupied France to oppose the Germans. They hid Jews, spied on the Germans, and sent vital information to the Allies. They helped more than 2,000 Allied airmen who landed in enemy territory to escape. They carried secret weapons such as silent pistols, bombs hidden inside common objects, and suicide tablets that looked like coat buttons, which they could swallow in case of capture.

June 13

Germans launch 10 pilotless V-1 rockets from the coast of France toward London. Although only one reaches London, it is the start of another devastating blitz against Britain that lasts for the rest of the war.

LIBERATION
IN SIGHT

April

The Luftwaffe uses the first jet-engine aircraft in war. Until now all planes had propellers.

July 18

Losses in China, as well as the loss of the island of Saipan on July 9, force Japan's Prime Minister Tojo to resign.

July 20

Colonel Claus von Stauffenberg, a respected German military officer, plants a bomb in a meeting room at Hitler's headquarters, Wolf's Lair, in eastern Germany. The bomb explodes, but does not harm Hitler. Stauffenberg and others are executed the next day. Resistance groups inside Germany had been trying to overthrow Hitler, and previous assassination attempts had also failed.

1944

Code breakers at Bletchley Park in England use the Colossus calculating machine, an early computer, to break down coded German messages. American code breakers learn Japanese codes, helping to shorten the war.

July 21

U.S. troops begin landing on Guam. Japanese resistance there ends in August, but fighting continues in the jungles of Burma, other Pacific Islands, and at sea.

July 23

Majdanek in Poland is the first concentration camp to be liberated, by Soviet troops.

July 25

The Allies begin Operation Cobra. American forces advance from Normandy to circle behind the German Army and take them from the rear. Bombers, tanks, and infantry lead the charge.

Aug. 25

The Allies liberate Paris.

Sept. 13

U.S. troops reach the Siegfried Line, a line of defensive forts and antitank traps on the border between France and Germany. Two days later the Rhineland Campaign, a push to the heart of Germany, begins.

Aug. 15

In Operation Dragoon the Allies land in southern France and travel north. It convinces Hitler to withdraw his troops from Normandy so they can return to Germany before being cut off from the south.

Sept. 17–25

Operation Market-Garden is fought when British and American ground and airborne troops attempt to cross the Rhine and cut off the German Army in the Netherlands. Despite freeing much of the Netherlands, the attack ultimately fails to reach its goals.

DESPERATE MEASURES

Oct. 14

Hitler accuses General Rommel of taking part in the July 20 assassination plot. Rommel can choose trial or suicide. He chooses suicide. There is no evidence that Rommel betrayed Hitler.

Oct. 16

The Soviet Army crosses into Prussia, a region in northeast Germany.

1944

Oct. 20

U.S. forces land in the Philippines. After fierce fighting, the Allies defeat the Japanese at the Battle of Leyte Gulf on Oct. 26. The Japanese, desperate to win, begin kamikaze attacks. Kamikazes, planes packed with explosives, dive directly into U.S. ships and sink them. Kamikaze pilots vow to die for Japan.

Nov. 23

French troops liberate Strasbourg, France.

Nov. 2

Canadian forces capture the last corner of Belgium from the Germans.

Nov. 24

More than 100 U.S. B-29 Superfortresses bomb an aircraft factory in Tokyo.

Dec. 5–6

U.S. forces begin the final offensive against Japanese troops in the Philippines.

Hitler plans a winter offensive against the Allies in Belgium. He takes the Allies by surprise at the Battle of the Bulge. The Germans begin strong, but after three days, their tanks run out of fuel and the Allies blow up bridges to prevent German retreat. The Allies claim victory, but both sides suffer serious losses. About 80,000 Allied troops and up to 100,000 German troops are killed or wounded.

B-29 SUPERFORTRESS

The first B-29 Superfortress aircrafts reached Allied airfields in India and China in April 1944. B-29s were the largest bombers in the war. They had four propellers and flew at 30,000 feet (9,144 meters), out of reach of Japanese aircraft. Their maximum speed was 357 miles per hour (575 kph). B-29s were armed with 10 machine guns, a cannon in the tail, and 20,000 pounds (9,072 kilograms) of bombs. They were crucial to winning the Pacific war.

German soldier in Belgium

MOUNTING
DEATH TOLLS

Jan. 17

Soviet troops liberate
Warsaw. They reach
Auschwitz on Jan. 27
and liberate the
concentration camp.

Feb. 4

Churchill, Roosevelt, and Stalin (from left) meet at
Yalta in the Crimea. They plan how to divide Europe
after victory.

(1945)

Jan. 28

Allies reopen the Burma
Road, a major supply
route in southern China.

Hitler surveys
bombing damage

Feb. 13–15

Nearly 800 RAF and U.S. planes bomb Dresden,
Germany, creating a firestorm that destroys
the city and kills an estimated 25,000 people.
In coming weeks and months, the Allies bomb
Magdeburg, Nuremberg, Würzburg, Dortmund,
Berlin, and many smaller cities in Germany.
Hundreds of thousands of civilians die and
German transportation is severely disrupted.

slave laborers at Buchenwald

April

The Allies liberate Buchenwald and Belsen concentration camps. On April 29 the 32,000 survivors of Dachau are freed by American forces.

April 12

President Roosevelt dies of a heart attack. Vice President Harry Truman becomes president, but doesn't learn about the Manhattan Project until April 25.

April 29

German forces in Italy surrender to the Allies.

Feb. 19–March 26

U.S. Marines land on the tiny Japanese-held island of Iwo Jima. The Allies want to set up an airfield as a base for bombing Japan. The Japanese put up a strong defense using a network of underground passages that makes them seem invisible. The Japanese hold out for more than a month. The Marines win at a high cost—one out of every three is either killed or wounded in the battle.

March 9–10

More than 300 U.S. B-29s bomb Tokyo, killing more than 100,000 people, leaving 1 million homeless, and burning about 16 square miles (41 sq. km) of the city.

April 1

American troops land on Okinawa, a Japanese island. A bloody three-month battle ensues before the Americans defeat the Japanese.

April 27

Mussolini tries to escape to Switzerland but is captured by Italian resistance fighters. They kill him the next day in Mezzegra, Italy.

April 30

Hitler commits suicide in Berlin as the Soviet Army closes in.

FINAL DAYS

Field Marshal Wilhelm Keitel signs Germany's surrender.

May 2
The Soviets take control of Berlin after intense fighting.

May 7
Germany surrenders to the Allies.

May 4
German forces in the Netherlands, Denmark, and northwest Germany surrender to the Allies.

May 8
Celebrations mark VE (Victory in Europe) Day.

June 6
The Allies carve Germany into four zones to be occupied by the Soviet Union, the U.S., Great Britain, and France.

June 21
U.S. forces capture Okinawa.

July 5
General MacArthur declares the Philippines liberated.

July 17–26
Churchill, Stalin, and Truman meet at Potsdam, Germany, to work out the terms of peace. They agree to disarm Germany, disband the German military, and forbid weapons manufacturing. They will arrest and try German war criminals and form new borders between Germany, Poland, and the Soviet Union. During the conference Churchill is replaced by Clement Atlee as prime minister following the recent British general election.

1945

July 26

The Allies demand that Japan surrender. Japan refuses. The Japanese Army broadcasts this message to its soldiers: "We shall fight on to the bitter end, ever firm in our faith that we shall find life in death … and surge forward to destroy the arrogant enemy!"

Aug. 8

The Soviet Union enters the war against Japan and attacks Japanese forces in China and Korea.

Nov. 14

The Nuremberg trials begin in Germany to bring Nazi leaders to justice for their acts against the Jewish people and others killed in death camps.

Aug. 6

A U.S. B-29 bomber drops the first atomic bomb on Hiroshima, Japan. Three days later pilots drop a second bomb on Nagasaki. At least 100,000 people die in each attack; many more will suffer long-term effects. The bombings lead to Japan's surrender.

Aug. 14

Japan surrenders. The world celebrates VJ (Victory in Japan) Day on Aug. 15. But even after the surrender, fighting continues. The Soviet Army claims victory in Manchuria on Aug. 23.

Oct. 9

Japan chooses Kijuro Shidehara as prime minister dedicated to peace.

Dec. 6

U.S. Congress approves a $3.75 billion loan to Great Britain to rebuild the British economy. The U.S. will also aid other countries.

RECOVERING FROM WAR

READ MORE

Chrisp, Peter. *World War II: Fighting for Freedom: The Story of the Conflict that Changed the World 1939–1945.* New York: Scholastic, 2010.

Huey, Lois Miner. *Voices of World War II: Stories from the Front Lines.* Mankato, Minn.: Capstone Press, 2011.

Miller, Terry. *D-Day: The Allies Strike Back During World War II.* New York: Franklin Watts, 2010.

Nardo, Don. *Hitler in Paris: How a Photograph Shocked a World at War.* North Mankato, Minn.: Compass Point Books, 2014.

INTERNET SITES

Use FactHound to find Internet sites related to this book.
All of the sites on FactHound have been researched by our staff.

Here's all you do:

Visit www.facthound.com

Type in this code: 9781476541587

INDEX